6 Ways To Create Generational Wealth

And How To Pass It Down To Your Kids

The six key strategies for creating and preserving generational wealth

BY BONIFACE MUTUA MUTHII

6 Ways To Create Generational Wealth And How To Pass It Down To Your Kids

The six key strategies for creating and preserving generational wealth

By Boniface Mutua Muthini

Copyright & Disclaimer

Table of Contents

Preface

"Generational wealth" is a term that many of us have heard, but few truly understand. In its simplest form, it is the accumulation of financial resources and assets that are passed down from one generation to the next, providing financial security and opportunities for future generations. It is about creating a legacy that can make a positive impact on your family and community for years to come.

In this book, "6 Ways To Create Generational Wealth And How To Pass It Down To Your Kids" we delve into the key components of creating and preserving wealth for future generations. We will share valuable lessons learned from some of history's most successful families and provide you with actionable strategies that you can implement in your own wealth-building journey.

We will explore the importance of mindset, timing, habits, compounding, strategy and relationships in creating a successful wealth-building strategy. We will also provide examples of how these strategies have been successfully implemented by other families in the past.

Whether you're just starting to think about building wealth for future generations or you're well on your way, this book will provide you with the guidance and insights you need to take your wealth-building efforts to the next level.

So, if you're ready to learn how to create a legacy of wealth for your family that can last for generations, let's dive in and explore the six key strategies for creating and preserving generational wealth.

Introduction

Are you looking to build a legacy of wealth for your family that can last for generations? If so, you're in the right place. In this book, we'll delve into the key components of creating and preserving generational wealth, and share some of the most valuable lessons we've learned from some of history's most successful families.

But before we dive into the specifics, let's define exactly what we mean by "generational wealth." Simply put, it's the accumulation of financial resources and assets that are passed down from one generation to the next, often with the intention of providing financial security and opportunities for future generations. It's about more than just accumulating wealth for personal gain; it's about creating a legacy that can make a positive impact on your family and community for years to come.

So, how can you create and pass down generational wealth to your children and grandchildren? Here are six key strategies to consider:

1. **Mindset**: The way you think about money and wealth plays a huge role in your ability to create and preserve it. Cultivate a growth mindset, embrace learning and personal development, and be open to new ideas and opportunities.
2. **Timing**: Timing is everything when it comes to building wealth. Keep an eye on economic trends and try to anticipate opportunities before they happen.
3. **Habits**: Successful wealth-building requires discipline and consistent effort. Develop good financial habits, such as saving and investing consistently, and avoid bad habits that can derail your efforts.
4. **Compounding**: The power of compound interest can't be overstated. By starting to save and invest early, and continuing to do so over time, you can maximize the growth of your wealth.
5. **Strategy**: A solid wealth-building strategy is essential. This could include a diverse portfolio of investments, a clear plan for saving and budgeting, and a focus on long-term growth.
6. **Relationships**: Building strong relationships with trusted advisors, such as financial planners and attorneys, can help you navigate the complexities of building and preserving wealth.

Now that we've covered the basic principles of creating and preserving generational wealth, let's look at some real-life examples of families who have done just that.

One classic example is the Medici family, a powerful banking dynasty in Renaissance Italy. The Medicis were known for their financial acumen and their willingness to invest in and support the arts, science, and education. Through their patronage of great minds like Leonardo da Vinci and Michelangelo, the Medicis helped to shape the cultural and intellectual landscape of their time, and their legacy of wealth and influence continues to this day.

Another notable example is the Carnegie family, whose wealth was built on Andrew Carnegie's success in the steel industry. Carnegie believed in the power of education and philanthropy to create positive change, and he used his wealth to fund the construction of thousands of libraries around the world. His legacy lives on through the Carnegie Corporation, which continues to fund educational and charitable causes to this day.

These are just a few examples of the many families throughout history who have used their wealth to create a lasting legacy. By learning from their successes and challenges, and applying the principles we've outlined above, you too can build and pass down a legacy of wealth to your children and grandchildren.

In this book, we've outlined six key strategies for creating and preserving generational wealth: mindset, timing, habits, compounding, strategy, and relationships. In the following chapters, we'll delve into each of these strategies in greater detail, and provide practical tips and examples to help you apply them in your own wealth-building journey.

Chapter 1: Mindset

Your mindset plays a crucial role in your ability to create and preserve wealth. If you have a fixed mindset, believing that your financial success is determined by external factors or your inherent abilities, you may be less likely to take risks or pursue new opportunities. On the other hand, if you have a growth mindset, believing that you can improve and grow through learning and effort, you'll be more open to new challenges and more likely to take the steps needed to build wealth.

To cultivate a growth mindset, try adopting some of the following practices:

- Embrace learning and personal development. Seek out new knowledge and experiences, and be open to trying new things.
- Seek out mentors and advisors who can provide guidance and support.
- Practice gratitude and focus on the things you have, rather than dwelling on what you lack.
- Set goals for yourself, and take small steps to achieve them. Celebrate your progress along the way.

Embrace learning and personal development

Embracing learning and personal development is an important aspect of cultivating a growth mindset and building wealth. When you are open to learning new things and constantly seeking to improve yourself, you are more likely to be open to new opportunities and challenges. This can help you grow both personally and financially, and set you up for long-term success.

Here are a few ways in which learning and personal development can help you create and preserve wealth:

- ☐ **Improved skills and knowledge**: By continuously learning and developing new skills, you can increase your value as an employee or business owner and position yourself for higher paying job opportunities or promotions. You may also be able to use your newfound knowledge and skills to start your own business or invest in new ventures.

- ☐ **Enhanced problem-solving and decision-making abilities**: Learning and personal development can help you improve your critical thinking and decision-making skills, which can be invaluable in managing your finances and making informed investment decisions.

- ☐ **Greater adaptability**: In a constantly changing world, the ability to adapt and learn new things is essential for long-term success. By embracing learning and personal development, you can stay ahead of the curve and be better equipped to navigate changing economic conditions and market shifts.

- ☐ **Increased confidence and motivation**: When you are constantly learning and improving yourself, you may feel more confident and motivated to pursue your goals. This can be especially important when it comes to building wealth, as it can take time and effort to achieve financial success.

By embracing learning and personal development, you can cultivate a growth mindset and set yourself up for long-term financial success. This can not only benefit you personally, but also help you pass down your knowledge and skills to future generations, enabling them to create and preserve wealth for themselves.

One example of how embracing a growth mindset can lead to wealth creation is the story of self-made billionaire, Elon Musk. Musk, who is now known for his successful ventures in companies like Tesla and SpaceX, didn't always have an easy path to success. He faced numerous setbacks and failures along the way, but instead of letting these setbacks define him, he used them as opportunities to learn and grow. He remained focused on his goals and never gave up, even when things looked bleak. This persistence and willingness to learn and adapt is a key part of Musk's success and is a testament to the power of a growth mindset.

Seek out mentors and advisors

Another way to cultivate a growth mindset is to surround yourself with successful and inspiring people. This can help you learn from their experiences, challenge your own beliefs and assumptions, and push yourself to be better. For example, if you want to build wealth through real estate investing, seek out successful real estate investors and ask them for advice and mentorship. By surrounding yourself with these types of role models, you can learn from their successes and mistakes and apply that knowledge to your own wealth-building journey.

Seeking out mentors and advisors can be an invaluable step in building and preserving wealth. These individuals can provide guidance, support, and insights that can help you navigate the complex world of finance and achieve your long-term goals.

Here are a few ways in which mentors and advisors can help you create and preserve wealth:

☐ **Provide guidance and support**: Mentors and advisors can offer guidance and support as you pursue your financial goals. They can help you develop a clear plan for building wealth, and provide encouragement and motivation when you face challenges or setbacks.

☐ **Offer insights and advice**: Mentors and advisors who have experience in the financial industry can provide valuable insights and advice that can help you make informed decisions about your finances. This can include recommendations for investments, strategies for saving and budgeting, and advice on how to build and preserve wealth.

☐ **Share their expertise and knowledge**: Mentors and advisors can share their expertise and knowledge with you, helping you learn new things and develop your own skills and knowledge in the process. This can be especially valuable if you are just starting out on your wealth-building journey and are looking to learn from those who have already achieved financial success.

☐ **Introduce you to new opportunities**: Mentors and advisors who have a wide network of contacts may be able to introduce you to new opportunities that can help you grow your wealth. This could include introductions to potential business partners, investors, or clients.

By seeking out mentors and advisors who can provide guidance and support, you can tap into the expertise and knowledge of others to help you create and preserve wealth over the long term.

Practice gratitude and focus on what you have

Practicing gratitude can help you maintain a positive and growth-oriented mindset. When you focus on the things you have, rather than dwelling on what you lack, you'll be more likely to feel content and motivated to take action. To practice gratitude, try keeping a gratitude journal, where you write down a few things you're grateful for each day. This can help you shift your focus from negative thoughts to positive ones, and can have a profound impact on your mindset and overall outlook.

Practicing gratitude and focusing on the things you have can be an important aspect of cultivating a growth mindset and building wealth. When you are grateful for what you have and focus on the positive aspects of your life, you may be more likely to feel motivated and inspired to pursue your goals.

Here are a few ways in which practicing gratitude and focusing on the things you have can help you create and preserve wealth:

- **Increased motivation and positivity**: When you are grateful for the things you have, you may be more motivated to work hard and pursue your goals. This can be especially important when it comes to building wealth, as it can take time and effort to achieve financial success. Focusing on the positive aspects of your life can also help you stay positive and motivated, even when you face challenges or setbacks.

- **Greater appreciation for the value of money**: When you focus on the things you have, rather than dwelling on what you lack, you may gain a greater appreciation for the value of money. This can help you make more mindful and informed decisions about your finances, and encourage you to be more mindful about how you spend and save.

- **Improved relationships and social connections**: Focusing on the things you have and being grateful for them can help you build stronger relationships and social connections. When you are grateful and positive, you may be more likely to attract positive and supportive people into your life, which can be valuable when it comes to building and preserving wealth.

By practicing gratitude and focusing on the things you have, you can cultivate a growth mindset and set the stage for long-term financial success. This can not only benefit you personally, but also help you pass down a positive and grateful attitude to future generations, enabling them to create and preserve wealth for themselves.

Set goals and take the steps to achieve them

In addition to seeking out mentors and role models, it's also important to regularly set and work towards financial goals. This helps you stay focused and motivated, and gives you something to strive for. When setting financial goals, it's important to be specific and make them achievable, yet challenging. For example, instead of simply setting a goal to "save more money," set a specific target, like "save $10,000 in the next 12 months." This goal is specific, measurable, attainable, relevant, and time-bound, which makes it more likely to be achieved.

Setting goals for yourself and taking small steps to achieve them is an important aspect of cultivating a growth mindset and building wealth. By setting clear and specific goals, you can give yourself a roadmap for success and stay focused on what you want to achieve.

Here are a few ways in which setting goals and taking small steps to achieve them can help you create and preserve wealth:

- **Increased motivation and focus:** By setting clear goals for yourself, you can give yourself a sense of purpose and motivation to work towards something specific. This can help you stay focused and engaged in your wealth-building efforts, and give you a sense of accomplishment as you make progress towards your goals.

- **Improved planning and organization:** Setting goals can help you create a plan for how you will achieve them, breaking down larger objectives into smaller, more manageable steps. This can help you stay organized and on track, and can make it easier to track your progress and make adjustments as needed.

- **Greater flexibility and adaptability:** By setting smaller, intermediate goals, you can give yourself the flexibility to adjust your plan as needed. This can be especially important when it comes to building wealth, as you may encounter unexpected challenges or opportunities along the way. By setting smaller goals, you can be more agile and adaptable as you work towards your long-term objectives.

By setting goals for yourself and taking small steps to achieve them, you can cultivate a growth mindset and set the stage for long-term financial success. This can not only benefit you personally, but also help you pass down a goal-oriented attitude to future generations, enabling them to create and preserve wealth for themselves.

Chapter 2: Timing

Timing is a crucial factor in building wealth. By anticipating economic trends and identifying opportunities before they happen, you can position yourself to take advantage of them. This requires a combination of research, analysis, and intuition.

Some strategies for maximizing the timing of your wealth-building efforts include:

- Keep an eye on economic indicators, such as interest rates, inflation, employment data, and stock market trends.
- Look for industries or sectors that are poised for growth, and consider investing in companies or assets that stand to benefit from these trends.
- Be ready to pivot if your current investments or strategies aren't performing as expected. Don't be afraid to sell and move on to new opportunities if necessary.
- Consider the long-term outlook, rather than just focusing on short-term gains. Building wealth is a marathon, not a sprint.

Timing is an important factor in building and preserving wealth. While it's important to start saving and investing as early as possible, it's also crucial to be strategic about when you make your moves. For example, if you're planning to buy a house, it may make sense to wait until the housing market is favorable to buyers. Or, if you're planning to invest in stocks, you may want to consider the overall state of the economy and the potential for growth.

One way to stay attuned to changes in the market and make smart timing decisions is to regularly review your financial situation and goals, and be ready to adjust your strategy as needed. This might involve reallocating your investments, paying off debt, or making other changes to your financial plan.

It's also important to be aware of the potential risks and rewards associated with different investments, and to make decisions that align with your risk tolerance and long-term goals. For example, if you're planning for retirement and are looking for more stable investments, you may want to consider options like bonds or mutual funds. On the other hand, if you're willing to take on more risk in exchange for the potential for higher returns, you may want to consider options like individual stocks or real estate.

In addition to staying attuned to changes in the market and being strategic about your investments, it's also important to consider the tax implications of your financial decisions. For example, if you're planning to sell a piece of real estate, you'll want to consider the tax implications of the sale, and whether it makes sense to hold onto the property for a longer period of time to potentially reduce your tax burden. By understanding the tax implications of your financial decisions, you can make more informed choices and potentially save money in the long run.

Consider the overall state of the economy and the potential for growth

By keeping an eye on economic indicators, such as interest rates, inflation, employment data, and stock market trends, you can gain a better understanding of the current economic environment and make more informed decisions about your finances.

Here are a few ways in which keeping an eye on economic indicators can help you create and preserve wealth:

- **Improved investment decisions**: By staying up to date on economic indicators, you can gain insight into trends and patterns that may influence the performance of different investments. This can help you make more informed decisions about where to allocate your money, and can help you minimize risk and maximize returns.

- **Better planning for the future**: By understanding the current economic environment, you can make more informed decisions about your long-term financial plans. For example, if you know that interest rates are likely to rise in the coming years, you may want to consider locking in a fixed-rate mortgage or refinancing your current loan to take advantage of lower rates.

- **Greater flexibility and adaptability**: By staying aware of economic trends and indicators, you can be more agile and adaptable in your financial planning. This can help you make adjustments as needed, and can enable you to take advantage of opportunities as they arise.

By keeping an eye on economic indicators and staying informed about the current economic environment, you can improve your timing and make more informed decisions about your finances. This can be especially important when it comes to building and preserving wealth, as it can help you minimize risk and maximize returns over the long term.

Look for industries or sectors that are poised for growth

One way to improve your timing is to look for industries or sectors that are poised for growth. By identifying trends and sectors that are likely to see increased demand or expansion in the future, you can position yourself to take advantage of these opportunities and potentially increase your wealth.

Here are a few ways in which looking for industries or sectors that are poised for growth can help you create and preserve wealth:

- **Improved investment returns**: By investing in companies or assets that stand to benefit from growth in a particular industry or sector, you can potentially earn higher returns on your investment. For example, if you identify an industry that is expected to see significant growth in the coming years, you may want to consider investing in companies that operate within that sector.

- **Increased diversification**: By investing in a variety of industries and sectors, you can diversify your portfolio and reduce risk. This can be especially important in times of economic uncertainty, as it can help you weather downturns and maintain your wealth over the long term.

- **Greater flexibility and adaptability**: By keeping an eye on trends and sectors that are poised for growth, you can be more agile and adaptable in your investment strategy. This can enable you to take advantage of new opportunities as they arise, and can help you stay ahead of the curve in terms of your financial planning.

By looking for industries or sectors that are poised for growth, and considering investing in companies or assets that stand to benefit from these trends, you can improve your timing and potentially increase your wealth. This can be an important part of building and preserving wealth for yourself and for future generations.

Be ready to pivot if your current investments or strategies aren't performing as expected

Being ready to pivot when your current investments or strategies aren't performing as expected can be an important part of good timing. By being willing to sell and move on to new opportunities when necessary, you can minimize losses and position yourself to take advantage of new opportunities as they arise.

Here are a few ways in which being ready to pivot can help you create and preserve wealth:

- **Reduced risk**: By being willing to sell investments that aren't performing as expected, you can minimize potential losses and reduce your overall risk profile. This can be especially important in times of economic uncertainty, as it can help you protect your wealth and avoid unnecessary risks.

- **Improved returns**: By staying nimble and being willing to pivot when necessary, you can potentially increase your returns by taking advantage of new opportunities as they arise. For example, if you see an industry or sector that is poised for growth, you may want to consider investing in companies or assets that stand to benefit from these trends.

☐ **Greater flexibility and adaptability**: By being ready to pivot, you can be more flexible and adaptable in your investment strategy. This can help you stay ahead of the curve and take advantage of new opportunities as they arise, rather than being stuck with investments or strategies that aren't working out.

By being ready to pivot when necessary, you can improve your timing and increase your chances of success when it comes to building and preserving wealth. This can be an important part of a long-term financial plan, and can help you maximize your returns and minimize risk over the long term.

Considering the long-term outlook over short-term gains

When it comes to building and preserving wealth, it's important to consider the long-term outlook, rather than just focusing on short-term gains. This is because building wealth is a marathon, not a sprint, and it requires a long-term perspective to be successful.

Here are a few reasons why a long-term outlook is important when it comes to creating and preserving wealth:

☐ **Compounding returns**: Many investments, such as stocks and mutual funds, have the potential to compound over time. This means that the returns on these investments can increase over time, as the value of the investments increases. By focusing on the long-term, you can take advantage of the power of compounding and potentially increase your wealth over time.

☐ **Risk management:** Focusing on the long-term can also help you manage risk, as you're less likely to panic and make impulsive decisions when markets are volatile. By staying invested for the long haul, you can potentially weather short-term market fluctuations and come out ahead in the end.

☐ **Ability to weather setbacks**: Building wealth is rarely a straight line, and there will inevitably be ups and downs along the way. By focusing on the long-term, you can take a more measured approach and be better able to weather setbacks and recover from any losses you may incur.

By considering the long-term outlook when it comes to building and preserving wealth, you can increase your chances of success and potentially maximize your returns over the long run. This can be an important part of a successful financial plan, and can help you achieve your financial goals over time.

Chapter 3: Habits

Creating and preserving wealth requires discipline and consistent effort. To be successful, you'll need to develop good financial habits and avoid bad ones.

Some habits that can help you build wealth include:

- Saving and investing consistently. Start by setting aside a portion of your income each month, and consider setting up automatic investments to make the process easier.
- Paying off debt. High-interest debt, like credit card debt, can eat away at your wealth. Prioritize paying off these debts as quickly as possible.
- Living below your means. Don't spend more than you earn, and try to save and invest as much as you can.
- Seeking out new opportunities for growth and learning. Don't be afraid to try new things and take calculated risks.

On the other hand, habits to avoid include:

- Overspending and living beyond your means. This can lead to debt and financial instability.
- Procrastinating on financial planning. The sooner you start saving and investing, the more time you'll have for your money to grow.
- Ignoring your investments. Don't forget to review your portfolio and make adjustments as needed.
- Being too risk-averse. While it's important to be cautious, don't let fear hold you back from pursuing growth opportunities.

Developing good financial habits is a crucial component of building and preserving wealth. These habits might include saving a certain percentage of your income, paying off debt, investing in your education, or regularly reviewing your financial plan. By cultivating these habits, you'll be better able to build and maintain wealth over the long term.

Saving and investing consistently

One habit that can be especially helpful in building wealth is saving a portion of your income on a regular basis. This might involve setting aside a certain percentage of your paycheck each month, or setting a specific savings goal and working towards it. By saving consistently, you'll be better able to weather financial setbacks and have a cushion to fall back on in case of emergencies.

Saving and investing consistently means setting aside a portion of your income on a regular basis and investing it in a variety of assets, such as stocks, bonds, mutual funds, and real estate. By saving and investing consistently, you can build a solid foundation for your financial future and increase your wealth over time.

Here are a few reasons why saving and investing consistently is important when it comes to creating and preserving wealth:

- **Compounding returns**: As mentioned earlier, many investments have the potential to compound over time, meaning that the returns on these investments can increase as the value of the investments increases. By saving and investing consistently, you can take advantage of the power of compounding and potentially increase your wealth over time.

- **Ability to weather setbacks**: Building wealth is rarely a straight line, and there will inevitably be ups and downs along the way. By saving and investing consistently, you'll be better able to weather setbacks and recover from any losses you may incur.

- **Peace of mind**: Finally, saving and investing consistently can provide peace of mind, knowing that you're taking steps to secure your financial future and protect yourself and your loved ones from financial insecurity.

By making saving and investing a consistent part of your financial plan, you can increase your chances of building and preserving wealth over the long run. This can be an important step in achieving your financial goals and building a solid foundation for your financial future.

Paying off debt

Another helpful habit is paying off debt. If you have high-interest credit card debt or other types of debt, it can be tempting to just make the minimum payments each month. However, this can result in paying much more in interest over time. Instead, try to pay off as much debt as possible as quickly as you can, or consider consolidating your debt to potentially reduce the interest rate.

High levels of debt can be a drain on your financial resources and limit your ability to invest and grow your wealth. By paying off debt, you can free up more money to put towards savings and investments, which can help you build and preserve wealth over time.

There are a few key strategies you can use to pay off debt:

- **Create a budget**: One of the first steps to paying off debt is to get a clear understanding of your income and expenses. By creating a budget, you can identify areas where you can cut back on spending and redirect those funds towards paying off debt.

- **Prioritize high-interest debt**: If you have multiple debts, it's often a good idea to focus on paying off the ones with the highest interest rates first. This will help you save money on interest in the long run and can help you pay off your debts more quickly.

- **Consider consolidation**: If you have multiple debts with different interest rates, you may be able to save money by consolidating them into one loan with a lower interest rate. This can make it easier to manage your debts and pay them off more quickly.

- **Seek out professional help**: If you're struggling to get your debts under control, consider seeking out professional help. A financial planner or a credit counselor can help you develop a plan to pay off your debts and get back on track.

By paying off debt and reducing your financial obligations, you'll be in a better position to save and invest, which can help you create and preserve wealth over the long term.

Living below your means

Living below your means is another key habit to consider when it comes to building and preserving wealth. Essentially, this means spending less money than you earn, and saving or investing the difference. By living below your means, you can build up a financial cushion that can help you weather economic downturns, pay for unexpected expenses, or fund long-term goals like retirement or your children's education.

There are a few key strategies you can use to live below your means:

- **Create a budget**: One of the first steps to living below your means is to get a clear understanding of your income and expenses. By creating a budget, you can identify areas where you can cut back on spending and redirect those funds towards saving and investing.

- **Look for ways to save money**: There are many different ways to save money, from cutting back on unnecessary expenses to shopping around for the best prices on goods and services. By looking for ways to save money, you can free up more money to put towards your long-term financial goals.

- **Automate your savings**: By setting up automatic transfers from your checking account to your savings or investment accounts, you can make sure you're saving consistently and not relying on your willpower to make it happen.

- **Invest in your earning power**: Another way to live below your means is to invest in your earning power. This could mean going back to school to get a higher degree, learning new skills, or starting a side hustle to generate additional income.

By living below your means, you'll be in a better position to save and invest, which can help you create and preserve wealth over the long term.

Continuously learning and improving your skills

Investing in your education is another habit that can help you build wealth. By continuously learning and improving your skills, you'll be better able to position yourself for career advancement and higher earning potential. This might involve taking classes, earning additional certifications, or networking with other professionals in your field.

In today's rapidly changing economy, it's more important than ever to stay current and adapt to new technologies and changing market conditions. By continuously learning and improving your skills, you can:

- **Increase your earning power**: By learning new skills or obtaining additional education, you may be able to qualify for higher paying jobs or negotiate a higher salary. This can help you increase your income and, in turn, your ability to save and invest.

- **Stay competitive in the job market**: By continuously learning and improving your skills, you'll be better equipped to compete for jobs and promotions in your field. This can help you advance your career and increase your earning potential over the long term.

- **Prepare for changes in your industry**: By staying up to date with the latest developments in your field, you'll be better prepared for changes in your industry. For example, if your industry is adopting new technologies, learning about those technologies can help you stay ahead of the curve and remain competitive.

- **Enhance your problem-solving and decision-making skills**: Learning and improving your skills can also help you develop your problem-solving and decision-making abilities. These skills are valuable in any career and can help you make better financial decisions, which can lead to greater wealth over time.

There are many different ways to learn and improve your skills, from taking classes or earning a higher degree, to reading books or attending workshops. By making a commitment to continuous learning, you'll be better positioned to create and preserve wealth over the long term.

.

Regularly review your financial plan and make adjustments

Finally, it's important to regularly review your financial plan and make adjustments as needed. This might involve setting new goals, reallocating your investments, or making other changes based on your current situation and long-term objectives. By regularly reviewing your plan, you'll be able to ensure that your financial strategy is still aligned with your goals and that you're making progress towards achieving them.

Regularly reviewing your financial plan and making adjustments is an important habit to develop when it comes to creating and preserving wealth. By reviewing your plan on a regular basis, you'll be able to assess your progress, identify any areas where you may be falling short, and make any necessary adjustments to get back on track. Some key things to consider when reviewing your financial plan include:

- ☐ **Your savings and investment goals**: Are you on track to reach your savings and investment goals? If not, you may need to make adjustments to your budget or increase your contributions.

- ☐ **Your debt**: Are you making progress on paying off your debt? If not, you may need to consider ways to cut expenses or increase your income to pay off your debt more quickly.

- ☐ **Your insurance coverage**: Do you have sufficient insurance coverage to protect your assets and your family in the event of a disaster or unexpected event? If not, you may need to review your insurance policies and make changes to ensure that you're adequately covered.

- ☐ **Your estate plan**: Do you have a will, power of attorney, and other necessary documents in place to protect your assets and ensure that they pass to your loved ones as you wish? If not, you may need to work with an attorney to create these documents.

By regularly reviewing your financial plan, you'll be able to make any necessary adjustments to ensure that you're on track to reach your wealth-building goals. This can help you create and preserve wealth for you and your loved ones.

Seeking out new opportunities for growth and learning

Seeking out new opportunities for growth and learning is an important habit to develop when it comes to creating and preserving wealth. By continually learning and improving your skills, you'll be better equipped to take advantage of new opportunities as they arise. Some ways to seek out new opportunities for growth and learning include:

- **Learning new skills**: Consider taking classes or workshops to learn new skills that can help you build wealth. For example, you might take a course on investing, financial planning, or entrepreneurship to learn more about these subjects and gain valuable skills.

- **Networking**: Attend events and join groups where you can meet people who are knowledgeable about wealth-building strategies. These connections can provide valuable insights and opportunities for growth.

- **Reading and staying up-to-date**: Read books and articles about wealth-building strategies, and stay up-to-date on economic and financial news. This can help you learn about new opportunities and be prepared to take advantage of them when they come along.

- **Seeking out mentors**: Find someone who has already achieved success in building wealth, and ask for their guidance and support. A mentor can provide valuable insights and advice, and help you stay on track as you work towards your wealth-building goals.

By seeking out new opportunities for growth and learning, you'll be better equipped to create and preserve wealth for you and your loved ones.

Chapter 4: Compounding

Compound interest is the concept that the interest you earn on your investments can be reinvested and earn additional interest, leading to exponential growth over time. The earlier you start saving and investing, and the more consistent you are, the more you'll benefit from the power of compound interest.

To take advantage of compound interest, try these strategies:

- Start saving and investing as early as possible. The earlier you start, the more time you'll have for your money to grow.
- Invest in assets that offer the potential for compound interest, such as stocks, mutual funds, or real estate.
- Consider setting up automatic investments to make the process easier and more consistent.
- Don't withdraw your investments too frequently, as this can reduce the power of compound interest.

Compounding is the process of generating returns on both your principal investment and the accumulated returns from previous periods. This means that as your investment grows, the returns on that investment also grow, leading to exponential growth over time.

To illustrate the power of compounding, consider the following example: if you invest $100 at a 10% annual return, after one year you'll have $110. If you leave the $110 in the investment and earn another 10% return the following year, you'll have $121. But if you continue to earn 10% returns each year, by the end of year 10, your investment will have grown to $259. This is because the returns from each year are being reinvested and earning additional returns in the following years.

There are several ways to take advantage of the power of compounding to build wealth. One of the most important is to start investing as early as possible. The earlier you start, the more time you'll have for compound growth to work its magic. For example, if you start investing $500 per year at age 25 and earn an 8% annual return, you'll have $406,000 by the time you reach 65. But if you wait until age 35 to start investing, you'll only have $246,000 by age 65, despite investing the same amount of money each year.

Another way to maximize the benefits of compounding is to choose investments with high returns. While it's important to be mindful of risk, choosing investments with the potential for higher returns can help you achieve faster compound growth. It's also important to be consistent with your investments, as this can help you take full advantage of compound growth over time. For example, if you're able to consistently invest $500 per year over a 40-year period and earn an 8% annual return, you'll have over $1 million by the end of that period.

Start saving and investing as early as possible

One of the key principles of building wealth is to start saving and investing as early as possible. This is especially important when it comes to creating generational wealth, as you'll be able to pass your wealth down to your children and future generations. Here are some reasons why starting early is so important:

- Time is your ally when it comes to building wealth. The earlier you start saving and investing, the more time you'll have for your money to grow. This is especially important when it comes to compound interest, which can lead to exponential growth in your wealth over time.

- By starting to save and invest early, you'll be able to take advantage of opportunities that may not be available later on. For example, you may be able to invest in high-growth companies or sectors when they are still in their early stages, which can lead to significant returns over time.

- Starting early also allows you to take on more risk in your investments, as you'll have more time to weather any market ups and downs. This can be especially important when it comes to building generational wealth, as you'll need to be able to withstand the ups and downs of the market over a long period of time.

By starting early, you'll be able to take advantage of compound interest, seize opportunities, and be able to withstand market fluctuations over the long term.

Invest in assets that offer the potential for compound interest

Investing in assets that offer the potential for compound interest is a key strategy for creating wealth. Compounding is the process by which interest earned on an investment is reinvested, thus earning interest on the interest. This can lead to exponential growth in the value of the investment over time. Here are some reasons why it's important to invest in assets that offer the potential for compound interest:

- Allows for exponential growth in the value of the investment over time. For example, if you invest $10,000 at an annual interest rate of 7% and leave it invested for 30 years, it will grow to over $81,000.

- Can create wealth for yourself and future generations. By investing in assets that offer compound interest and leaving your investment untouched, you can watch your money grow over time and create wealth for yourself and future generations.

- Diversifies your investment portfolio and reduces risk. By investing in a variety of assets, you are less likely to suffer significant losses if any one investment performs poorly.

☐ Can be a powerful tool for building wealth over the long term. Compound interest works best when invested for a longer period of time, the longer you invest the more the compound interest will benefit you.

By investing in assets that offer the potential for compound interest, you can watch your money grow over time and create wealth for yourself and future generations.

Consider setting up automatic investments

Setting up automatic investments is a great way to take advantage of the power of compounding to create wealth. Here are some reasons why it's important to consider setting up automatic investments:

☐ **Establishes a consistent savings plan**: By setting up automatic investments, you can ensure that a certain amount of money is invested on a regular basis. This can help establish a consistent savings plan and make it easier to reach your financial goals over time.

☐ **Takes advantage of dollar-cost averaging**: By investing a fixed amount of money on a regular basis, you can take advantage of dollar-cost averaging. This is a strategy where you buy more shares of an investment when the price is low and fewer shares when the price is high. This can help reduce the impact of market fluctuations on your investments over time.

☐ **Avoids procrastination and forgetfulness**: Setting up automatic investments can help you avoid procrastination and forgetfulness. It eliminates the need to manually initiate investments and ensure that you don't miss any investment opportunities.

☐ **Takes advantage of the power of compounding**: Automatic investments can help you take full advantage of the power of compounding by allowing your money to grow at a faster rate over time. The more consistent and regular you invest, the more your money grows.

☐ **Helps to create generational wealth**: Automatic investments can help to create wealth for yourself and future generations by consistently growing your investments over time.

Overall, setting up automatic investments can be a great way to take advantage of the power of compounding to create wealth for yourself and future generations.

Don't withdraw your investments too frequently

Not withdrawing your investments too frequently is an important aspect of taking advantage of the power of compounding to create wealth. Here are some reasons why it's important to not withdraw your investments too frequently:

- **Allows compounding to occur**: By not withdrawing your investments too frequently, you allow compounding to occur. Compounding means that the interest earned on an investment is reinvested, earning interest on the interest. This leads to exponential growth in the value of the investment over time.

- **Reduces the impact of taxes and fees**: Withdrawing your investments too frequently can lead to higher taxes and fees. By not withdrawing your investments too frequently, you can reduce the impact of taxes and fees on your overall returns.

- **Avoids market timing mistakes**: Withdrawing your investments too frequently can lead to market timing mistakes. By not withdrawing your investments too frequently, you can avoid the temptation to sell your investments at the wrong time, which can lead to poor returns.

- **Helps to create generational wealth**: Not withdrawing your investments too frequently can help to create wealth for yourself and future generations by consistently growing your investments over time.

- **Allows to reach your financial goals**: By not withdrawing your investments too frequently, you can reach your financial goals faster, whether it is for retirement, buying a house or starting a business.

Overall, not withdrawing your investments too frequently is an important aspect of taking advantage of the power of compounding to create wealth for yourself and future generations.

Chapter 5: Strategy

Developing a solid wealth-building strategy is essential to creating and preserving generational wealth. This should include a diverse portfolio of investments, a clear plan for saving and budgeting, and a focus on long-term growth.

To build a successful wealth-building strategy, consider the following steps:

- Create a financial plan. This should include a budget, a savings plan, and a long-term investment strategy.
- Diversify your investments. Don't put all your eggs in one basket. Consider a mix of stocks, bonds, real estate, and other assets to reduce risk.
- Seek out professional advice. Consider working with a financial planner or advisor to help you make informed decisions about your investments.
- Review your strategy regularly. As your financial situation and goals change, be sure to adjust your strategy accordingly.

Developing a well-thought-out investment strategy is an important part of creating and preserving wealth. This involves considering your financial goals, risk tolerance, and investment time horizon, and choosing investments that align with these factors.

One key aspect of investment strategy is asset allocation, which refers to the mix of different types of investments in your portfolio. Different types of assets, such as stocks, bonds, and cash, tend to perform differently in different market conditions, and choosing the right mix of assets can help you achieve your financial goals while minimizing risk.

For example, if you're saving for a short-term goal, such as a down payment on a home, you might choose a more conservative asset allocation with a higher proportion of cash and fixed income investments, as these tend to be less volatile than stocks. On the other hand, if you're saving for a long-term goal, such as retirement, you might choose a more aggressive asset allocation with a higher proportion of stocks, as these tend to have higher potential returns over the long term.

Another key aspect of investment strategy is diversification, which refers to spreading your investments across different asset classes and industries. This can help minimize risk by reducing the impact of any single investment on your overall portfolio. For example, if you have a portfolio that's heavily invested in tech stocks and the tech sector experiences a downturn, your portfolio will likely be impacted more significantly than if you had diversified your investments across multiple sectors.

Developing a solid investment strategy can be a complex process, and it's often helpful to work with a financial advisor or professional to create a plan that aligns with your financial goals and risk tolerance. By taking the time to carefully consider your investment strategy, you'll be better equipped to create and preserve wealth over the long term.

Create a financial plan

Creating a financial plan that includes a budget, a savings plan, and a long-term investment strategy is a critical aspect of a successful wealth-building strategy. Here are some reasons why it's important to create a financial plan:

- **Helps to set clear financial goals**: A financial plan helps you to set clear financial goals and to determine the steps necessary to reach them. This can include short-term goals such as paying off debt or building an emergency fund, as well as long-term goals such as retirement planning or saving for a child's education.

- **Helps to prioritize spending**: A budget is a key component of a financial plan. It helps you to prioritize spending and to identify areas where you may be overspending. By creating a budget, you can ensure that your spending aligns with your financial goals and that you're saving enough to reach them.

- **Helps to build a savings plan**: A savings plan is a critical component of a financial plan. It helps you to set aside money for short-term and long-term goals, such as saving for an emergency fund, retirement or a down payment on a house.

- **Helps to create a long-term investment strategy**: A long-term investment strategy is an important aspect of a financial plan. It helps you to choose the right investments to achieve your financial goals and to diversify your portfolio to reduce risk.

- **Helps to create generational wealth**: By creating a financial plan and following it, you can create wealth for yourself and future generations. A financial plan helps to ensure that you're saving and investing enough to reach your financial goals and to build wealth over time.

In conclusion, a comprehensive financial plan that takes into account all aspects of one's financial life is crucial for successful wealth building. This includes creating a budget to prioritize spending, setting up a savings plan to reach short-term and long-term goals and developing a long-term investment strategy to grow wealth over time. By having a clear and well-executed plan in place, it not only helps to achieve individual financial goals but also creates wealth for future generations.

Diversify your investments

Diversifying your investments is an important aspect of a successful wealth-building strategy. By diversifying your investments, you can reduce risk and increase the chances of achieving your financial goals. Here are some reasons why it's important to diversify your investments:

- **Reduces risk**: Diversifying your investments helps to reduce risk by spreading your money across different types of assets. This means that if one investment performs poorly, the others may perform well, helping to offset any losses.

- **Helps to balance your portfolio**: Diversifying your investments helps to balance your portfolio by allocating your assets in a way that aligns with your investment goals and risk tolerance.

- **Helps to take advantage of different market conditions**: Diversifying your investments allows you to take advantage of different market conditions. By investing in a variety of assets, you can benefit from the growth potential of one asset while also being protected from the downturns of another.

- **Helps to create a mix of income streams**: Diversifying your investments helps to create a mix of income streams. This can include stocks, bonds, real estate, and other assets that can provide you with regular income.

- **Helps to create generational wealth**: Diversifying your investments can help to create wealth for yourself and future generations by providing a mix of assets that can grow over time and provide a source of income.

Overall, diversifying your investments and considering a mix of stocks, bonds, real estate, and other assets is an important aspect of a successful wealth-building strategy and can help to reduce risk and create wealth for yourself and future generations.

Seek out professional advice

Seeking out professional advice and working with a financial planner or advisor is an important aspect of a successful wealth-building strategy. Here are some reasons why it's important to seek professional advice:

- **Helps you to understand your financial situation**: A financial planner or advisor can help you to understand your current financial situation and to identify any areas where you may need to make changes. They can help you to create a financial plan and to set realistic financial goals.

- **Helps you to make informed investment decisions**: A financial planner or advisor can help you to make informed investment decisions. They can help you to choose the right investments for your risk tolerance and investment goals. They can also help you to diversify your investments and to create a balanced portfolio.

- **Helps you to navigate complex financial issues**: A financial planner or advisor can help you to navigate complex financial issues such as taxes, estate planning, and retirement planning. They can help you to understand the implications of different financial decisions and to make the best choices for your unique situation.

- **Helps you to stay on track**: A financial planner or advisor can help you to stay on track with your financial plan and to make adjustments as needed. They can also help you to monitor your progress and to make sure that you're on track to reach your financial goals.

- **Helps to create generational wealth**: A financial planner or advisor can help to create wealth for yourself and future generations by providing guidance and advice on investment strategies and financial planning.

Overall, seeking out professional advice and working with a financial planner or advisor is an important aspect of a successful wealth-building strategy and can help to create wealth for yourself and future generations by providing guidance and advice on investment strategies and financial planning.

Review your strategy regularly

Reviewing your wealth-building strategy regularly is an important aspect of a successful wealth-building strategy. Here are some reasons why it's important to review your strategy regularly:

- **Helps to adapt to changes in your financial situation**: As your financial situation changes, it may require changes to your wealth-building strategy. Reviewing your strategy regularly allows you to make adjustments as needed, to ensure that your strategy aligns with your current financial situation and goals.

- **Helps to take advantage of new opportunities**: The financial landscape is constantly changing, and new opportunities may arise. Reviewing your strategy regularly helps you to identify new opportunities that align with your financial goals and adapt your strategy to take advantage of them.

- **Helps to stay on track with your goals**: Reviewing your strategy regularly allows you to monitor your progress and ensure that you are on track to reach your financial goals. If you are not making progress, you can make adjustments to your strategy to get back on track.

- **Helps to identify and address potential risks**: Regularly reviewing your strategy can help you to identify and address potential risks, such as market changes or personal financial issues. This can help to reduce the impact of these risks on your wealth-building strategy.

- **Helps to create Generational wealth**: Reviewing your strategy regularly helps to create wealth for yourself and future generations by ensuring that your strategy aligns with your current financial situation and goals and that you are on track to reach your financial goals.

Overall, reviewing your wealth-building strategy regularly is an important aspect of a successful wealth-building strategy and can help to create wealth for yourself and future generations by adapting to changes in your financial situation, taking advantage of new opportunities, staying on track with your goals and identifying and addressing potential risks.

Chapter 6: Relationships

Building strong relationships with trusted advisors and professionals can be an essential component of creating and preserving generational wealth. These could include financial planners, attorneys, accountants, and other experts who can provide guidance and support as you navigate the complexities of wealth management.

To build strong relationships with advisors and professionals:

- Seek out advisors who have a track record of success and a good reputation. Look for recommendations from trusted sources, or do your own research to find advisors who seem like a good fit for your needs.
- Communicate clearly and openly with your advisors. Be honest about your financial situation and goals, and ask for help when you need it.
- Stay engaged with your advisors. Don't be afraid to ask questions or seek clarification on any issues that arise.
- Consider building relationships with multiple advisors in different areas of expertise. This can help you get a well-rounded perspective on your wealth-building efforts.

Building and maintaining positive relationships can be an important part of creating and preserving wealth. This includes seeking out mentors and advisors who can provide guidance and support, as well as surrounding yourself with like-minded individuals who share your financial goals and values.

One way to build positive relationships is to seek out mentors who can provide guidance and support as you work towards your financial goals. This might include seeking out a financial advisor or professional who can help you develop a solid investment plan, or finding a mentor who has experience in a specific industry or area of expertise that you're interested in. By seeking out mentors who can provide guidance and support, you'll be able to benefit from their knowledge and experience, and you'll have someone to turn to for advice and support as you navigate the financial world.

In addition to seeking out mentors, it's also important to surround yourself with like-minded individuals who share your financial goals and values. By forming relationships with people who prioritize financial responsibility and are open to discussing financial matters, you'll be more likely to stay on track and achieve your goals.

In addition to seeking out supportive relationships, it's also important to be mindful of the impact of your relationships on your financial situation. For example, if you're in a romantic relationship, it's important to have open and honest discussions about financial matters and to be on the same page when it comes to financial goals and priorities. This can help avoid misunderstandings and conflicts down the road, and can help you both work towards shared financial goals.

Overall, building and maintaining positive relationships can be an important part of creating and preserving wealth. By seeking out guidance and support from those around you, and being mindful of the impact of your relationships on your financial situation, you'll be better able to create and preserve wealth over the long term.

Seek out advisors who have a track record of success and a good reputation

Building strong relationships with trusted advisors and professionals is an important aspect of a successful wealth-building strategy. Here are some reasons why it's important to seek out advisors who have a track record of success and a good reputation:

- **Helps to ensure that you're working with experienced professionals**: Advisors who have a track record of success and a good reputation have likely been in the business for a while and have a lot of experience. They are more likely to have a deep understanding of the financial landscape and be able to provide you with the best advice for your situation.

- **Helps to ensure that you're working with reputable professionals**: Advisors who have a good reputation have likely earned it by providing high-quality service to their clients. They are more likely to be trustworthy and have your best interests at heart.

- **Helps to ensure that you're working with professionals who are held to a high standard**: Advisors who have a good reputation are likely held to a high standard by their clients and peers. They are more likely to be held accountable for their actions and to provide quality service.

- **Helps to ensure that you're working with professionals who are up-to-date with the latest trends and developments**: Advisors who have a track record of success and a good reputation are likely to be well-informed about the latest trends and developments in the financial landscape. They are more likely to be able to provide you with the most current and relevant advice to help you achieve your financial goals.

- **Helps to create Generational wealth**: Building strong relationships with trusted advisors and professionals that have a track record of success and a good reputation can help to create wealth for yourself and future generations by providing guidance and advice on investment strategies and financial planning. They can also help to ensure that your wealth is passed down to future generations in an efficient and effective manner. They can help in estate planning and tax planning which are important in ensuring that your wealth is passed on to future generations. Additionally, they can provide guidance and advice on how to best educate and empower future generations to manage their wealth and continue the legacy of creating wealth.

Overall, seeking out advisors who have a track record of success and a good reputation is an important aspect of building strong relationships with trusted advisors and professionals. It can help to ensure that you are working with experienced, reputable and well-informed professionals that can provide you with the best advice and guidance to achieve your financial goals and create wealth for yourself and future generations.

Communicate clearly and openly with your advisors

Communicating clearly and openly with your advisors is an important aspect of building strong relationships with trusted professionals and achieving a successful wealth-building strategy. Here are some reasons why it's important to communicate clearly and openly with your advisors:

- **Helps to establish trust**: By being honest about your financial situation and goals and asking for help when you need it, you can establish trust with your advisors. Trust is essential for building a strong relationship with your advisors and ensuring that they are able to provide you with the best advice and guidance.

- **Helps to ensure that your advisors understand your unique situation**: By communicating clearly and openly, your advisors can better understand your unique financial situation and goals. This can help them to provide you with advice and guidance that is tailored to your specific needs.

- **Helps to identify and address any issues**: By being honest about your financial situation, you can help your advisors to identify any issues that may need to be addressed. This can help to ensure that your wealth-building strategy is on track and that you are on track to reach your financial goals.

- **Helps to make informed decisions**: By asking for help when you need it, you can ensure that you are making informed decisions. Your advisors can provide you with the information you need to make informed decisions about your finances.

- **Helps to create Generational wealth**: By communicating clearly and openly with your advisors, you can create wealth for yourself and future generations. Your advisors can provide you with guidance and advice on investment strategies and financial planning that will help you to achieve your financial goals and create wealth for future generations.

Overall, communicating clearly and openly with your advisors is an important aspect of building strong relationships with trusted professionals and achieving a successful wealth-building strategy. It can help to establish trust, ensure that your advisors understand your unique situation, identify and address any issues, make informed decisions, and create wealth for yourself and future generations.

Stay engaged with your advisors

Staying engaged with your advisors is an important aspect of building strong relationships with trusted professionals and achieving a successful wealth-building strategy. Here are some reasons why it's important to stay engaged with your advisors:

- **Helps to ensure that you are informed**: By staying engaged with your advisors, you can ensure that you are informed about the latest trends, developments and changes in the financial landscape that may affect your wealth-building strategy.

- **Helps to keep your strategy on track**: By staying engaged with your advisors, you can monitor your progress and ensure that your wealth-building strategy is on track. You can also make adjustments as needed to reach your financial goals.

- **Helps to identify and address any issues**: By staying engaged with your advisors, you can identify and address any issues that may arise. This can help to ensure that your wealth-building strategy is on track and that you are on track to reach your financial goals.

- **Helps to make informed decisions**: By asking questions and seeking clarification on any issues that arise, you can make informed decisions about your finances. Your advisors can provide you with the information you need to make informed decisions.

- **Helps to create Generational wealth**: By staying engaged with your advisors, you can create wealth for yourself and future generations. Your advisors can provide you with guidance and advice on investment strategies and financial planning that will help you to achieve your financial goals and create wealth for future generations.

Overall, staying engaged with your advisors is an important aspect of building strong relationships with trusted professionals and achieving a successful wealth-building strategy. It helps to ensure that you are informed, keep your strategy on track, identify and address any issues, make informed decisions, and create wealth for yourself and future generations. Regular communication and engagement with your advisors allows you to stay up-to-date with the latest market trends and changes, and helps to ensure that your wealth-building strategy is aligned with your current financial situation and goals. Moreover, it also helps to build a strong and long-term relationship with your advisors, who can provide you with the right guidance and support throughout your wealth-building journey.

Consider building relationships with multiple advisors in different areas of expertise

Consider building relationships with multiple advisors in different areas of expertise is an important aspect of building strong relationships with trusted professionals and achieving a successful wealth-building strategy. Here are some reasons why it's important to consider building relationships with multiple advisors:

- **Helps to gain a well-rounded perspective on your wealth-building efforts**: By working with multiple advisors who specialize in different areas of expertise, you can gain a well-rounded perspective on your wealth-building efforts. This can help you to identify opportunities and make informed decisions about your finances.

- **Helps to manage risk**: By working with multiple advisors in different areas of expertise, you can gain a more comprehensive understanding of the risks associated with different investments and financial decisions. This can help you to create a diversified portfolio that balances risk and return.

- **Helps to access specialized knowledge**: By working with multiple advisors in different areas of expertise, you can access specialized knowledge and advice that can help you to achieve your financial goals.

- **Helps to ensure that you are getting the best advice**: By working with multiple advisors in different areas of expertise, you can ensure that you are getting the best advice and guidance for your specific needs.

- **Helps to create Generational wealth**: By working with multiple advisors in different areas of expertise, you can create wealth for yourself and future generations. Your advisors can provide you with guidance and advice on investment strategies and financial planning that will help you to achieve your financial goals and create wealth for future generations.

Overall, building relationships with multiple advisors in different areas of expertise is an important aspect of building strong relationships with trusted professionals and achieving a successful wealth-building strategy. It can help to gain a well-rounded perspective on your wealth-building efforts, manage risk, access specialized knowledge, ensure that you are getting the best advice and create wealth for yourself and future generations.

FREQUENTLY ASKED QUESTIONS

What is generational wealth and how do you build it?

What's the definition of generational wealth?

Generational wealth refers to the accumulation and preservation of wealth across multiple generations within a family. It is the transfer of financial resources, assets, and knowledge from one generation to the next, which can include things like property, investments, and businesses. The goal of building generational wealth is to provide future generations with a strong financial foundation and the means to achieve financial security and independence.

How do you build generational wealth?

Building generational wealth typically involves a combination of strategies, including:

- **Saving and investing wisely:** This includes setting financial goals, budgeting, and creating a plan to save and invest for the long-term. It may also involve seeking the advice of financial professionals to help identify the best investment opportunities.
- **Building and maintaining a strong credit score**: A good credit score can open up opportunities for borrowing and lending at favorable rates, which can help to grow wealth over time.
- **Starting and growing a business:** Building a successful business can provide a source of ongoing income, as well as opportunities for reinvestment and expansion.
- Building a diversified portfolio of assets: This can include a mix of assets such as stocks, bonds, real estate, and alternative investments. Diversifying assets can help to mitigate risk and increase the chances of generating returns over time.
- **Passing on knowledge and skills:** Teaching future generations about personal finance, investing, and other money management skills can help them make informed decisions and better manage their wealth.
- **Proper estate planning:** This includes creating a will and trust, and estate taxes to minimize taxes and maximize the wealth that can be passed on to future generations.

It's important to remember that building generational wealth takes time and requires a long-term perspective. It's also important to work with a team of financial professionals to ensure that your wealth is protected and managed effectively over the years.

Is generational wealth good?

The concept of generational wealth can be seen as both positive and negative, depending on one's perspective.

On the positive side, building and preserving wealth across multiple generations can provide a strong financial foundation for future generations, giving them the means to achieve financial security and independence. This can lead to improved opportunities for education, career advancement, and overall quality of life.

On the negative side, some argue that the concentration of wealth in a small number of families can contribute to economic inequality and limit opportunities for those without access to such wealth. Additionally, the accumulation of wealth over time can also perpetuate the cycle of privilege and disadvantage, where certain groups have more access to resources and opportunities than others.

It's important to keep in mind that how wealth is acquired, managed, and distributed also plays a role in determining whether it's considered good or bad. Wealth acquired through illegal or unethical means, as well as wealth that is hoarded and not used to benefit the community, is generally considered bad.

Ultimately, whether or not generational wealth is viewed as good or bad depends on the specific context and the values of the individuals and society involved.

What amount of money is considered generational wealth?

There is no specific dollar amount that defines "generational wealth," as the concept refers more to the transfer and preservation of wealth across multiple generations rather than a certain level of wealth. However, having a substantial amount of wealth is generally a prerequisite for building and preserving wealth over multiple generations. The threshold for what constitutes as substantial wealth can vary depending on the cost of living in a certain area or the lifestyle one wants to maintain.

In the United States, generally, a net worth of $10 million or more is considered to be in the top 0.1% of households in terms of wealth. However, this is not a hard and fast rule and the threshold may be different in other countries or regions.

It's important to remember that building and preserving wealth over multiple generations requires more than just having a large sum of money; it also involves strategies such as saving and investing wisely, building a strong credit score, starting and growing a business, building a diversified portfolio of assets, passing on knowledge and skills, and proper estate planning.

How much money does the average American inherit?

The amount of money that the average American inherits can vary greatly depending on a number of factors, including the individual's age, family circumstances, and the overall wealth of the estate.

According to a 2020 report from the Federal Reserve, the median inheritance received by American adults in 2020 was $64,000. The average inheritance amount was $295,000, but this number is skewed by a small number of very large inheritances.

It's worth noting that the inheritances are not equally distributed and a small percentage of Americans receive a large share of inherited wealth. According to the same report, the top 10% of Americans who received an inheritance in 2020 received an average of $1,081,000, while the bottom 50% received an average of $15,000.

Additionally, the inheritance received can also vary depending on the form it takes. Some inheritances may be in the form of cash, while others may be in the form of assets such as property or investments. In some cases, the inheritance may be in the form of a family business or other assets that can generate ongoing income.

It's also worth noting that the inheritances are not limited to cash or assets, it can also include knowledge, skills, and experience, which can provide a valuable foundation for building wealth over time.

It's important to remember that while inheritance can provide a significant financial boost, it should not be the sole focus of one's financial planning. Building a strong financial foundation through smart saving, investing, and budgeting can help to ensure financial security regardless of whether or not an inheritance is received.

HISTORY'S MOST SUCCESSFUL FAMILIES

History's most successful families in building and protecting generational wealth

What family has the most generational wealth?

There are many families around the world that have built and maintained substantial wealth over multiple generations. However, the family with the most wealth can vary depending on the time frame and the source of the information.

Some of the historical families that have been reported as having been successful in building and protecting generational wealth over the centuries include:

The Rothschild family: This European banking dynasty, founded by Mayer Amschel Rothschild in the 18th century, built a vast empire through smart investments, savvy business deals, and careful management of their wealth. They have been able to maintain their wealth and influence for over 250 years.

The Medici family: The Medici family of Florence, Italy, were successful merchants and bankers during the Renaissance. They used their wealth to patronize the arts, finance political and cultural projects, and support the Catholic Church. Their wealth and influence spanned over several generations and they are considered one of the most powerful families in European history.

The Fugger family: The Fugger family were a German merchant and banking family that became one of the wealthiest and most powerful families in Europe during the 16th century. They controlled vast business interests and were able to maintain their wealth and influence for several generations.

The Morgan family: The Morgan family, founded by the American financier J.P. Morgan, was one of the most powerful and wealthy families in the United States during the late 19th and early 20th centuries. They controlled a vast empire of banks, railroads, and industrial companies, and were able to maintain their wealth and influence for several generations.

The Ford family: The Ford family, founded by Henry Ford, built one of the most successful and innovative automobile companies in history. They were able to maintain their wealth and influence for several generations.

The Walton family: The descendants of Walmart founder Sam Walton are considered one of the wealthiest families in the world, with a combined net worth of over $200 billion.

The Koch family: The Koch brothers inherited their father's oil and gas company and have grown it into a vast conglomerate with interests in a wide range of industries.

The Mars family: The Mars family, known for their candy empire, is one of the wealthiest and most private families in the United States.

The Rockefeller family: The descendants of John D. Rockefeller, the founder of Standard Oil, are considered one of the wealthiest and most influential families in American history.

The Saudi Royal family: The Saudi Royal family has been known for its immense wealth **and** political power for decades.

It's worth noting that these are some examples of families that have been reported to have significant wealth, there are many other wealthy families that exist around the world. The ranking and net worth of these families can vary depending on sources and time frame. It's equally important to note that some of those families have achieved their wealth through unethical or illegal means, and their legacy can be seen as negative. Their wealth and influence also perpetuated the cycle of privilege and disadvantage, where certain groups have more access to resources and opportunities than others.

More About The Rothschild Family

The Rothschild family is a European banking dynasty that has been in existence for over 250 years and is considered one of the wealthiest and most powerful families in the world. The family's fortune was founded by Mayer Amschel Rothschild in the 18th century, who began as a money lender and then expanded his business into banking and finance. The family's wealth was built on a combination of smart investments, savvy business deals, and careful management of their wealth.

The Rothschild family's wealth and influence spread across Europe, with branches of the family establishing themselves in major financial centers such as London, Paris, and Frankfurt. They played a significant role in financing the industrial revolution, funding infrastructure projects, and investing in industries such as mining, railroads, and shipping. They also played a key role in the financial markets, acting as intermediaries in the issuance of government bonds and becoming one of the largest holders of government debt.

The Rothschilds were able to maintain their wealth and influence over several generations by keeping control of the family business within the family and by carefully managing their assets and investments. They also placed a strong emphasis on education and training future generations in the family business.

It's worth noting that the Rothschild family's wealth and influence has been a source of controversy, with some accusing the family of using their wealth and power to manipulate governments and financial markets to their advantage.

How did the Rothschilds become so wealthy?

The Rothschild family became one of the wealthiest and most powerful families in the world through a combination of smart investments, savvy business deals, and careful management of their wealth.

Mayer Amschel Rothschild, the founder of the Rothschild banking dynasty, began his career as a money lender and then expanded his business into banking and finance. He established a network of agents and correspondents across Europe, which allowed him to quickly and efficiently gather and disseminate information about financial and political developments. This gave the Rothschilds a significant advantage in the financial markets and allowed them to make informed investment decisions.

The Rothschilds also made significant investments in industries such as mining, railroads, and shipping, which helped to fuel the industrial revolution and generate substantial returns on investment. They also played a key role in the issuance of government bonds, acting as intermediaries between governments and investors and becoming one of the largest holders of government debt.

In addition to their business acumen, the Rothschilds were also known for their ability to maintain control of the family business within the family. They placed a strong emphasis on education and training future generations in the family business, which helped to ensure the continuity of the family's wealth and influence over several generations.

What do the Rothschilds own today?

Today, the Rothschild banking empire is not as centralized as it once was and there are multiple Rothschild-owned or controlled businesses, investment firms and charitable foundations across the globe. Some of the businesses and assets associated with the Rothschilds include:

- Rothschild & Co: This is a global investment bank that provides financial services such as investment banking, wealth management, and asset management.
- Waddesdon Manor: This is a National Trust property in the United Kingdom which was built by Baron Ferdinand de Rothschild in the late 19th century as a country retreat.
- Vineyards and wineries: The Rothschilds have been involved in the wine industry for over 200 years, owning vineyards and wineries in France, Italy, South Africa and Argentina
- Real estate: The Rothschilds have a wide range of real estate holdings, including properties in London, Paris, and other major cities around the world.
- Art and antiques: The Rothschilds have one of the world's most significant collections of art and antiques, which have been accumulated over several centuries.
- Philanthropy: The Rothschilds have also been involved in philanthropy for centuries, and have established foundations and charitable organizations to support education, the arts, and scientific research

It's worth noting that the Rothschilds are a private family and the extent of their wealth and assets is not fully disclosed. Additionally, the Rothschilds are not one entity, but a group of related families, each with its own business interests and investments.

More About The Medici Family

The Medici family was a powerful and influential banking and political dynasty in Florence, Italy, during the Renaissance period. They were one of the most prominent banking families in Europe and used their wealth to support the arts, finance political and cultural projects, and support the Catholic Church. They also held political power in the city-state of Florence and later in the Grand Duchy of Tuscany.

The family's fortune was founded by Giovanni di Bicci de' Medici, who established a successful banking business in the 14th century. His descendants, including Cosimo de' Medici and Lorenzo de' Medici, expanded the family's wealth and influence through a combination of banking, trade, and political power. They also made significant investments in the arts, supporting artists such as Botticelli, Michelangelo, and Leonardo da Vinci.

The Medici family was able to maintain their wealth and influence over several generations by keeping control of the family business within the family, and by carefully managing their assets and investments. They also placed a strong emphasis on education and culture, which helped to ensure the continuity of the family's wealth and influence.

The Medici family's legacy continues to be felt today, through their contributions to the arts and culture, their role in the development of banking and finance, and their impact on the politics and history of Florence and Italy.

How did the Medici become so wealthy?

The Medici family became one of the wealthiest and most powerful families in Europe during the Renaissance through a combination of banking, trade, and political power.

The family's fortune was founded by Giovanni di Bicci de' Medici, who established a successful banking business in the 14th century. He and his descendants provided financial services such as lending money to both individuals and city-states, as well as currency exchange, and deposit banking. The Medici bank also had a network of branches across Europe, which allowed them to quickly and efficiently gather and disseminate information about financial and political developments. This gave the Medici family a significant advantage in the financial markets and allowed them to make informed investment decisions.

The Medici family also made significant investments in trade, particularly in the wool industry, which generated substantial returns on investment. They also built a vast network of merchants and agents across Europe, which allowed them to control the trade of luxury goods such as silk, spices, and precious metals.

In addition to their business acumen, the Medici family also used their wealth and influence to gain political power in the city-state of Florence and later in the Grand Duchy of Tuscany. They supported the arts, financed political and cultural projects, and used their influence to promote their interests.

The Medici family was able to maintain their wealth and influence over several generations by keeping control of the family business within the family, and by carefully managing their assets and investments. They also placed a strong emphasis on education and culture, which helped to ensure the continuity of the family's wealth and influence.

What do the Medici own today?

The Medici family's wealth and influence has waned over the centuries and today there is not one specific entity that can be considered as "the Medici" that own any assets or businesses. The family's legacy, however, continues to be felt through the many cultural and architectural treasures they commissioned, donated and left behind in Florence, Tuscany and Italy.

- Many of the most famous art and architectural treasures of Florence, such as the Duomo, the Uffizi Gallery, and the Palazzo Medici Riccardi, were commissioned and/or financed by the Medici family.
- The Medici villas such as Villa La Petraia, Villa Medici, and Villa di Castello, are open to the public and are considered as important cultural and architectural heritage.
- The family's collection of art and antiques, which they accumulated over several centuries, is now housed in museums and galleries around the world.
- The Medici family also left behind a legacy of philanthropy, particularly in the areas of education and the arts, through the establishment of foundations and charitable organizations.
- The name Medici is still associated with luxury, culture, and heritage through various products and brands that use the name or the crest of the family.

It's worth noting that the legacy of the Medici family is not limited to tangible assets and cultural heritage, but also to the cultural and political impact they had on Florence and Italy. They were patrons of the arts and sciences, and their contributions to the development of banking and finance, as well as the support of the Catholic Church, have had a lasting impact on the culture and society of the Renaissance period and beyond.

More About The Fugger Family

The Fugger family was a German merchant and banking family that became one of the wealthiest and most powerful families in Europe during the 16th century. They controlled vast business interests and were able to maintain their wealth and influence for several generations. They were known for their ability to maintain control of the family business within the family, and by carefully managing their assets and investments. They also placed a strong emphasis on education and training future generations in the family business, which helped to ensure the continuity of the family's wealth and influence over several generations.

How did the Fugger become so wealthy?

The Fugger family's fortune was founded by Jakob Fugger, also known as Jakob Fugger the Rich, who began as a merchant and then expanded his business into banking and finance. He established a network of agents and correspondents across Europe, which allowed him to quickly and efficiently gather and disseminate information about financial and political developments. This gave the Fuggers a significant advantage in the financial markets and allowed them to make informed investment decisions. The Fuggers also made significant investments in industries such as mining, particularly in the silver mines of the Erzgebirge mountains, which generated substantial returns on investment. They also played a key role in the issuance of government bonds, acting as intermediaries between governments and investors and becoming one of the largest holders of government debt.

What do the Fugger own today?

Today, the Fugger family no longer exists as a unified entity and their wealth has been distributed among descendants and various branches of the family. There is not a specific business or asset that can be considered as "Fugger's". The Fugger name is still associated with banking, trade, and industry and is still a prominent name in Germany and Austria.

More About The Morgan Family

The Morgan family, founded by the American financier J.P. Morgan, was one of the most powerful and wealthy families in the United States during the late 19th and early 20th centuries. They controlled a vast empire of banks, railroads, and industrial companies, and were able to maintain their wealth and influence for several generations. J.P. Morgan himself was a prominent banker and businessman, known for his role in consolidating the American steel and railroad industries.

How did the Morgan Family become so wealthy?

The Morgan family's fortune was founded by J.P. Morgan, who began his career as a financier and then expanded his business into banking and industry. He played a key role in consolidating the American steel and railroad industries through a series of mergers and acquisitions, which generated substantial returns on investment. He also played a central role in the financial markets, acting as a trusted advisor to governments and other large corporations. He was known for his ability to raise large amounts of capital and his ability to navigate the complex financial landscape of the late 19th and early 20th centuries.

What do the Morgan Family own today?

Today, the Morgan family is still a prominent name in American business and finance, but is no longer a unified entity. The descendants of J.P. Morgan have diversified their investments and interests and don't have a specific business or asset that can be considered as "Morgan's". J.P. Morgan & Co., the bank founded by J.P. Morgan, is still in operation today as JPMorgan Chase, one of the largest banks in the United States and the world. The Morgan Library & Museum in New York

More About The Ford Family

The Ford family, founded by Henry Ford, built one of the most successful and innovative automobile companies in history, the Ford Motor Company. They were able to maintain their wealth and influence for several generations through the company's success. Henry Ford revolutionized the automobile industry with his development of the assembly line and the introduction of the Model T, which made cars more affordable and accessible to the masses. The company also played a significant role in the development of American industry, particularly in the areas of manufacturing and labor practices.

How did the Ford family become so wealthy?

The Ford family's fortune was founded by Henry Ford, who began his career as a mechanic and then expanded his business into the automobile industry. He revolutionized the automobile industry with his development of the assembly line and the introduction of the Model T, which made cars more affordable and accessible to the masses. This led to the tremendous growth of the Ford Motor Company, which generated substantial returns on investment for the Ford family. Additionally, Henry Ford was also known for his progressive labor policies, such as the $5 workday, which helped to attract and retain skilled workers, and improve productivity and efficiency.

What do the Ford family own today?

Today, the Ford family still owns a controlling interest in the Ford Motor Company, one of the largest and oldest car manufacturers in the world. The company is publicly traded and the Ford family is still involved in the company's management and operations through the Ford Family Trust, which owns the majority of the class B shares of the company. The family also has a philanthropic arm, the Ford Family Foundation, which focuses on improving the lives of people in the communities where Ford Motor Company operates.

More About The Walton Family

The Walton family, founded by Sam Walton, built one of the most successful retail companies in history, Walmart. They were able to maintain their wealth and influence for several generations through the company's success. Sam Walton founded Walmart in 1962, and through his innovative retailing concepts and a relentless focus on cost control, he built it into the largest retailer in the world. He and his family's wealth has been largely derived from Walmart, which is still one of the largest companies in the world by revenue.

How did the Walton family become so wealthy?

The Walton family's fortune was founded by Sam Walton, who began his career as a retail clerk and then expanded his business into discount retailing. He founded Walmart in 1962 and through his innovative retailing concepts, such as "Everyday Low Prices" and a relentless focus on cost control, he built it into the largest retailer in the world. This led to the tremendous growth of Walmart, which generated substantial returns on investment for the Walton family. Sam Walton also implemented a stock option program for employees, which allowed them to purchase shares in the company at a discount, further increasing the wealth of the family.

What do the Walton family own today?

Today, the Walton family still owns a controlling interest in Walmart, which is still one of the largest companies in the world by revenue. The company is publicly traded and the Walton family is still involved in the company's management and operations through the

Walton Family Trust, which owns the majority of the company's shares. The family also has a philanthropic arm, the Walton Family Foundation, which focuses on improving education, protecting the environment and promoting economic opportunity. The foundation has donated billions of dollars to various causes over the years.

More About The Koch Family

The Koch family is an American family that has built a significant business empire, primarily in the areas of energy, chemicals and finance. The family is best known for its ownership and control of Koch Industries, one of the largest privately held companies in the world. The Koch family is known for their conservative political views and has been influential in American politics through their philanthropy and advocacy for free market principles.

How did the Koch family become so wealthy?

The Koch family's fortune was founded by Fred C. Koch, who developed an oil refining process in the 1920s. He and his sons, Charles and David Koch, expanded the company into a diversified conglomerate, Koch Industries. They focused on building a portfolio of companies in a variety of industries, including oil, gas, refining, chemicals, and agriculture. They also made strategic acquisitions, such as the acquisition of Georgia-Pacific, a pulp and paper company, and INVISTA, a textile and polymer company. Koch Industries is one of the largest privately held companies in the world and generates substantial returns on investment for the Koch family.

What do the Koch family own today?

Today, the Koch family still owns a controlling interest in Koch Industries, a privately held conglomerate with diverse interests in various industries such as oil, gas, refining, chemicals, and agriculture. The company is still owned and controlled by the Koch family through the Koch family trust. The family also has a philanthropic arm, the Charles Koch Foundation, which focuses on promoting economic freedom, limited government and individual liberty. The foundation has donated billions of dollars over the years to various causes, including education, policy research, and advocacy groups that align with their political and economic beliefs. Additionally, the Koch family also has various investments in other businesses and industries, such as real estate, finance, and venture capital. They are known for their conservative political views, and have been influential in American politics through their philanthropy and advocacy for free market principles.

More About The Mars Family

The Mars family is an American family that has built a significant fortune through their ownership of Mars, Inc., one of the largest privately held companies in the world, and known for their confectionery and pet-food products, such as M&M's, Snickers, and Pedigree. The family is known for their secretive nature and keeping a low profile, however they are considered as one of the wealthiest families in the United States.

How did the Mars family become so wealthy?

The Mars family's fortune was founded by Frank C. Mars, who began his career as a candy maker and then expanded his business into confectionery. He developed the Milky Way bar in 1923 and later created the famous M&M's, which quickly became a popular treat. He also diversified into pet food, creating the K-9 meal for dogs and eventually led to the creation of the Pedigree dog food brand. The company was passed down to his children, Forrest Jr. and Jacqueline, who further expanded the business and diversified into other products such as Uncle Ben's Rice and Skittles. They focused on building a portfolio of confectionery and pet food brands, and have also made strategic acquisitions, such as Wrigley, a chewing gum company, and Banfield Pet Hospital. Mars, Inc. is one of the largest privately held companies in the world and generates substantial returns on investment for the Mars family.

What do the Mars family own today?

Today, the Mars family still owns a controlling interest in Mars, Inc., a privately held conglomerate with diverse interests in confectionery and pet food products. The company is still owned and controlled by the Mars family through a trust structure and is considered as one of the largest candy companies in the world. The family is known for their secretive nature, and they have a philanthropic arm, the Mars Foundation, which focuses on supporting education and environmental causes, but they keep the details of their charitable activities private.

More About The Rockefeller Family

The Rockefeller family is an American family that has built a significant fortune through their ownership of Standard Oil Company, one of the largest and most powerful companies in American history, and other business ventures. The family is known for their philanthropy, and for having a significant impact on American industry, politics and society, particularly in the late 19th and early 20th centuries.

How did the Rockefeller family become so wealthy?

The Rockefeller family's fortune was founded by John D. Rockefeller, who began his career as a bookkeeper and then expanded his business into the oil industry. He established Standard Oil Company in 1870 and through a series of strategic acquisitions, mergers and aggressive business practices, he built it into one of the largest and most powerful companies in American history. Standard Oil controlled nearly 90% of the oil refineries in the U.S and generated substantial returns on investment for the Rockefeller family. John D. Rockefeller was also known for his philanthropy, and he and his family established various foundations and charitable organizations that continue to support education, health and social welfare.

What do the Rockefeller family own today?

Today, the Rockefeller family fortune is managed by various trusts and foundations, and the family members have diversified their investments and interests. The Rockefeller Family Office still manages the family's investments and philanthropy, but there is no specific business or asset that can be considered as "Rockefeller's". The family's philanthropic efforts continue through various foundations such as the Rockefeller Foundation, which focuses on promoting the well-being of humanity throughout the world, and the Rockefeller Brothers Fund which focuses on advancing social change. The family is still considered as one of the wealthiest and most powerful families in the United States.

More About The Saudi Royal Family

The Saudi Royal Family is the ruling monarchy of Saudi Arabia, and has held political and economic power in the country for several decades. The country is known for its vast oil reserves, which have made it one of the wealthiest nations in the world. The Saudi Royal Family has used its control of the country's oil resources to amass a significant fortune and establish itself as one of the most powerful and influential families in the world.

How did the Saudi family become so wealthy?

The Saudi Royal Family's fortune was founded on the country's vast oil reserves, which were discovered in the 1930s. The family, under the leadership of King Abdulaziz Al Saud, established the Arabian American Oil Company (ARAMCO) which later became the Saudi Arabian Oil Company (Saudi Aramco) and is the state-owned oil company of Saudi Arabia. The company has a monopoly on oil production in the country and generates substantial returns on investment for the Saudi Royal Family. The family also has significant investments in other industries such as banking, real estate and construction.

What do the Saudi family own today?

Today, the Saudi Royal Family still holds significant control over the country's oil resources through Saudi Aramco, which is considered as the most profitable company in the world. The Saudi Royal Family also owns significant assets in various industries such as banking, real estate, construction, and media. The Saudi government also has a sovereign wealth fund, the Public Investment Fund (PIF), which is one of the largest sovereign wealth funds in the world and holds investments in a wide range of companies and industries. The Saudi Royal Family is considered as one of the wealthiest and most powerful families in the world.

FINAL THOUGHTS

Building wealth is a marathon, not a sprint

Building wealth is a long-term process that requires patience and discipline. It is not something that can be achieved overnight or through quick-fix solutions. Instead, building wealth is a marathon, a journey that requires consistent effort and focus over an extended period of time.

To build wealth, you must have a long-term mindset and be willing to make sacrifices in the short term to achieve your financial goals. This may mean saving and investing a portion of your income instead of spending it all on immediate pleasures, or taking on extra work or education to increase your earning potential.

Building wealth also requires consistent action over time. This means developing good financial habits, such as budgeting, saving, and investing, and sticking to them even when it's hard. It also means being proactive in seeking out opportunities to grow your wealth, whether through investing, entrepreneurship, or other means.

One of the most powerful tools for building wealth over the long term is compounding, which refers to the ability of an asset to generate earnings that are then reinvested to generate even more earnings. By starting to save and invest early and consistently, you can take advantage of the power of compounding to grow your wealth significantly over time.

Finally, building wealth requires a focus on long-term goals, rather than short-term gratification. It's important to have a clear vision of what you want to achieve financially, and to stay focused on that vision even when you face challenges or setbacks.

By embracing a long-term mindset and focusing on consistent action, good habits, and long-term goals, you can build wealth over the marathon of your lifetime. So, it is always better to start early and be consistent in your efforts towards building wealth.

Sarah's story about learning to create and preserve wealth

Sarah had always struggled with money. Growing up in a financially unstable household, she learned to be fearful of financial insecurity and believed that she would always struggle to make ends meet. She worked hard, but no matter how much she earned, it never seemed to be enough.

One day, Sarah ran into an old friend who had always seemed to have her life together. She was surprised to see how successful her friend had become financially and asked her how she had turned her financial situation around.

Her friend told her about the importance of having a growth mindset when it comes to wealth. She explained that by embracing learning and personal development, and being open to new ideas and opportunities, anyone could improve their financial situation. She encouraged Sarah to start reading books about personal finance and investing, and to attend financial seminars and workshops to learn more.

Sarah was skeptical at first, but decided to give it a try. She began reading books about investing and personal finance and attending financial seminars and workshops. She also sought out mentors and advisors who could provide guidance and support.

As Sarah began to adopt a growth mindset, her financial situation started to improve. She became more open to new opportunities and started taking calculated risks to grow her wealth. She also developed good financial habits, like budgeting and investing, which helped her make the most of her resources.

Over time, Sarah's financial situation continued to improve. She had built a solid financial foundation for herself and was well on her way to achieving her financial goals. Best of all, she was able to pass down her newfound knowledge and habits to her children, ensuring that they too would have the tools they needed to create and preserve wealth for future generations.

Sarah learned that with the right mindset and a willingness to learn and embrace new opportunities, it is possible to improve your financial situation and build wealth for future generations. She also learned the importance of developing good financial habits, such as budgeting and investing, and the power of compounding to grow wealth over time.

But Sarah also learned that building and preserving wealth is not just about mindset and habits. It also requires a focus on timing, strategy, and relationships. She learned to pay attention to the economic climate and make informed decisions about when to invest and when to hold onto her money. She also learned the importance of having a clear financial strategy and sticking to it.

But perhaps most importantly, Sarah learned that building and preserving wealth requires strong relationships. She sought out mentors and advisors who could provide guidance and support, and worked to cultivate strong relationships with her family and community. By seeking out guidance and support from those around her, and being mindful of the impact of her relationships on her financial situation, Sarah was able to create and preserve wealth over the long term.

Conclusion

In conclusion, creating and preserving wealth is a complex process that requires a combination of mindset, timing, habits, compounding, strategy, and relationships. By focusing on these key areas, you'll be better equipped to build and preserve wealth over the long term. Whether you're just starting out on your financial journey or you're well on your way to achieving your financial goals, taking the time to focus on these key areas can help you create and preserve wealth for generations to come.

Thank you

Dear Reader,

Thank you for taking the time to read my book, "6 Ways To Create Generational Wealth And How To Pass It Down To Your Kids." I hope that the information and insights shared in the book have been helpful to you in your journey towards creating wealth and passing it down to your future generations.

I would like to express my gratitude for your support and for giving me the opportunity to share my knowledge and experience with you. I am honored that you have chosen my book and I hope that it has provided you with valuable information and ideas on how to create wealth and preserve it for future generations.

I would love to hear your thoughts and feedback on the book. Your comments and suggestions are greatly appreciated, and will help me to continue to improve and provide valuable information in the future.

Thank you again for your support and for reading my book. I wish you all the best on your wealth-building journey.

Sincerely,

Boniface Mutua Muthini

About the author

Boniface Mutua Muthini is the author of "6 Ways To Create Generational Wealth And How To Pass It Down To Your Kids", a book that delves into the key components of creating and preserving wealth for future generations. With over 10 years of experience in the digital marketing and tech industry, Boniface specializes in business strategy and consulting. He has worked with a range of leading digital agencies, tech companies, real estate investment firms, wealth management companies, and business consulting firms, which has given him a wealth of knowledge and experience to share in his writing.

Boniface is also the author of other successful books such as "Business Strategy For Digital Service Businesses," which offers valuable insights and expertise to aid digital service businesses in achieving success, and "How To Start Your Digital Marketing Consultancy Business," a practical guide for aspiring digital marketing consultants.

Throughout his career, Boniface has worked with companies such as Extramiletech Systems, Dijidl Marketing, iPocket Marketing, Push Digital Media Ltd, Relentless Media Ltd, The Soho Loft, and RentIn Group Ltd (Vacation Rentals). His work with these digital marketing agencies has led to content strategy and marketing activities linked to major brands including ActionCOACH Franchise opportunities, Forbes, and VentureBeat.

Boniface brings a wealth of knowledge and experience to "6 Ways To Create Generational Wealth And How To Pass It Down To Your Kids," and he is excited to share his insights with readers. He hopes that his expertise will help guide individuals, investors and families towards success in creating and preserving wealth for future generations.

Made in the USA
Monee, IL
16 February 2023

27868974R00031